FOUR SEASONS
Coloring Book

100+ Unique Images.

Want a freebie?!
Sign Up Here

https://bridgetcoloringpress.com/free/

we'll send you something fun !!!

>>>>>>>>>>>>>>>>>>>>>>>>>>>>>>>>>>>

Share your art with us via
Instagram: @Bridgetcoloringpress
Facebook: @Bridgetcoloringpress

www.bridgetcoloringpress.com

For enquiries email us at

Support@bridgetcoloringpress.com

COLOR TEST PAGE

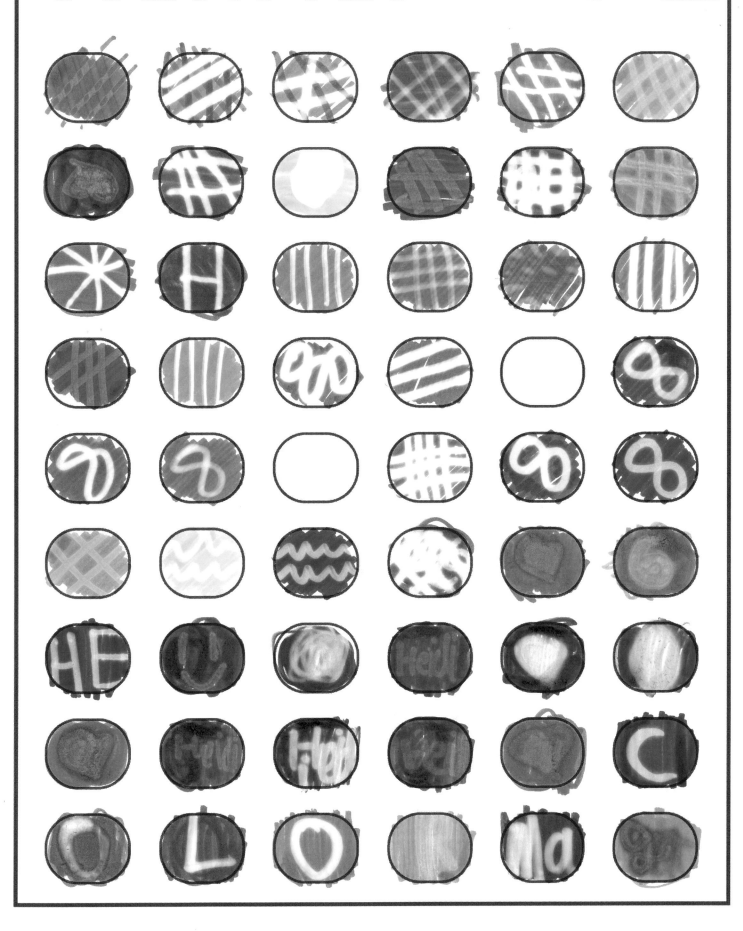

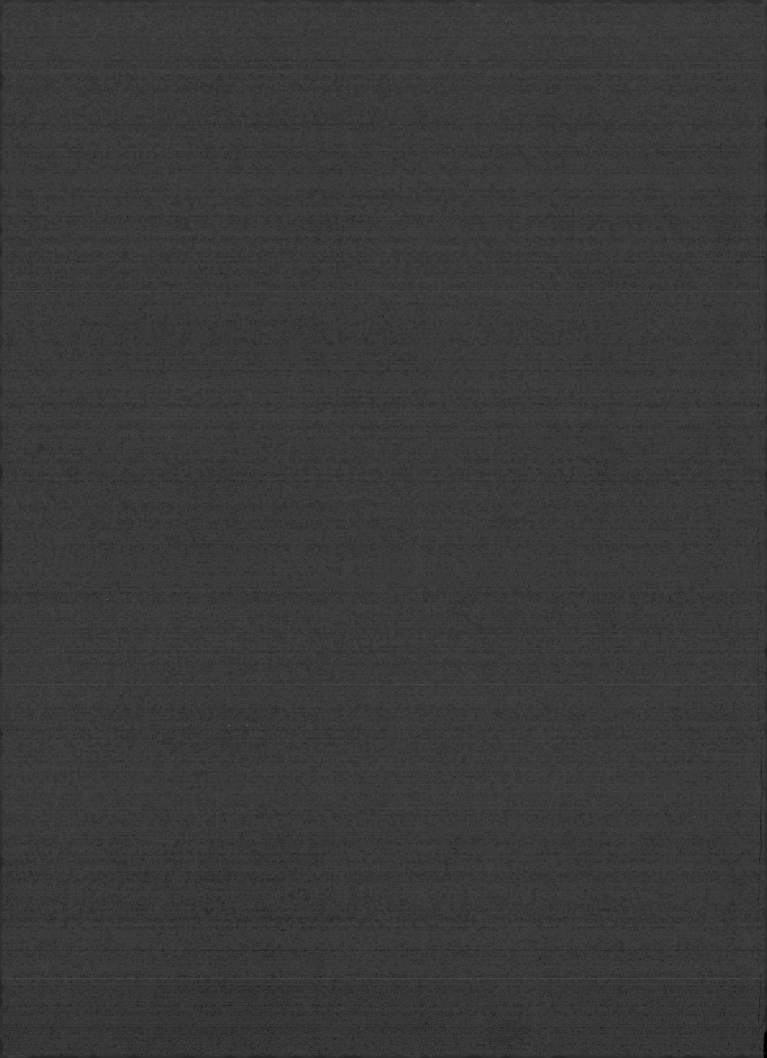

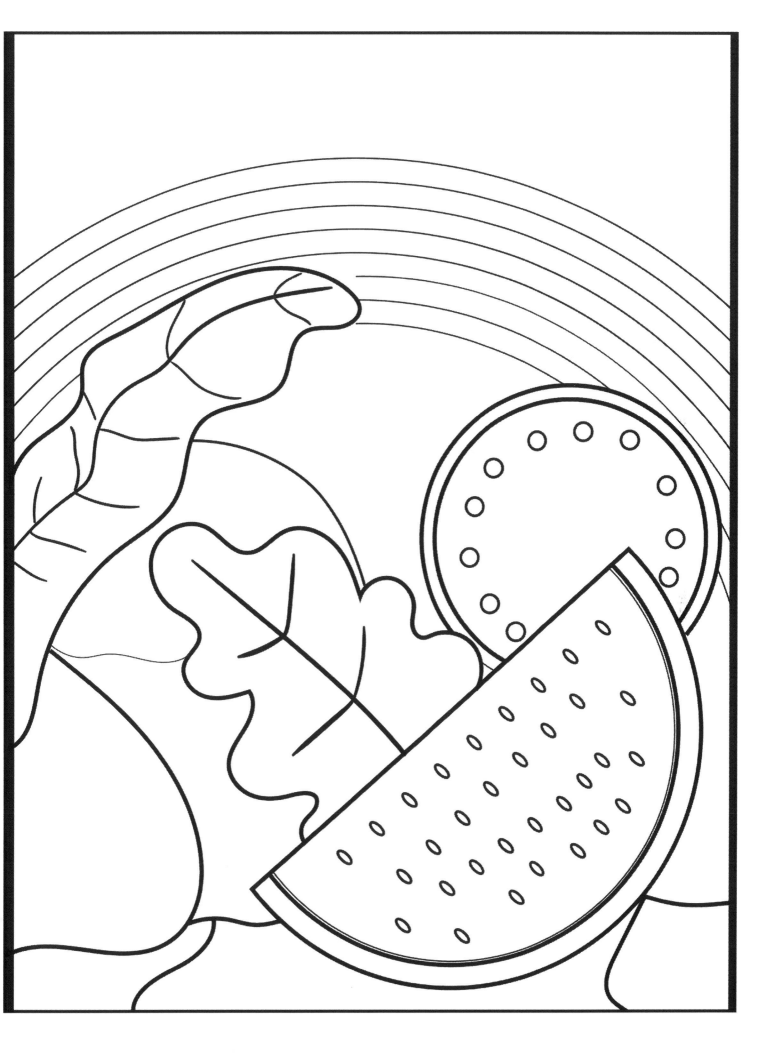

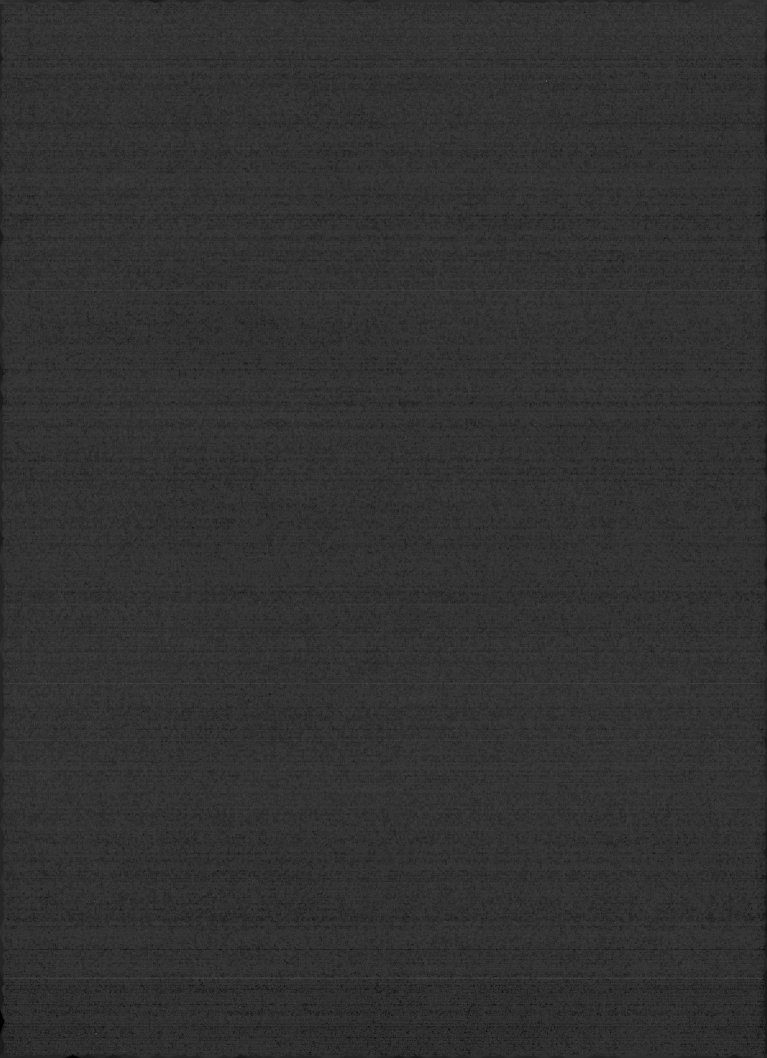

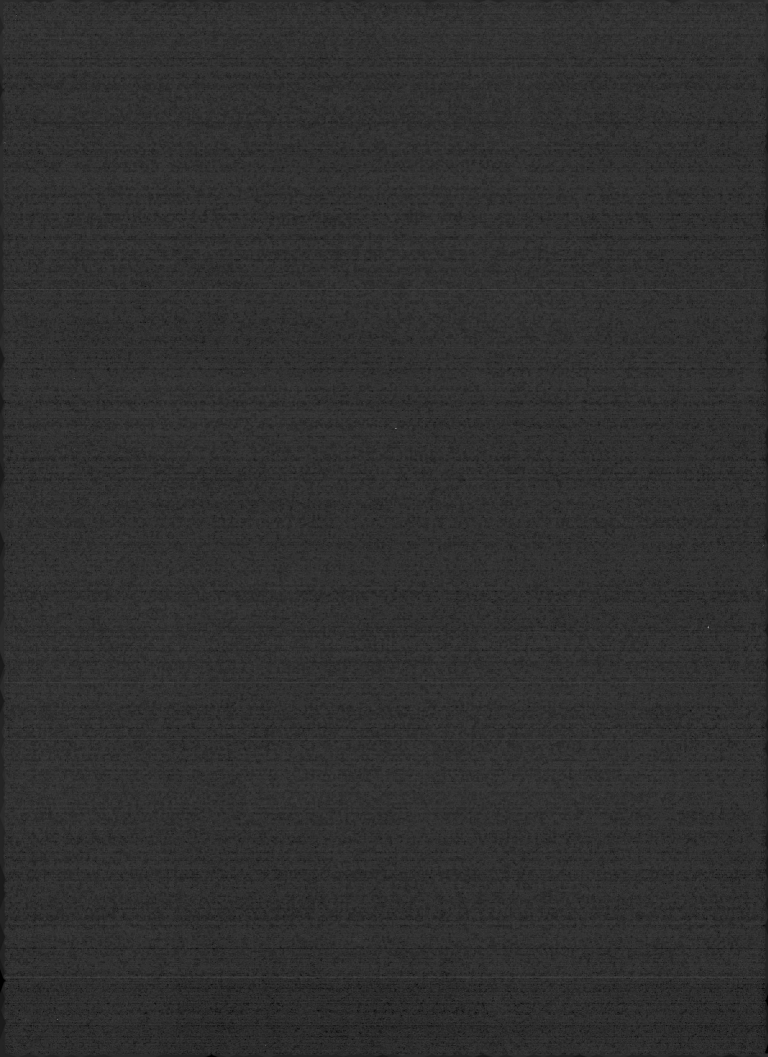

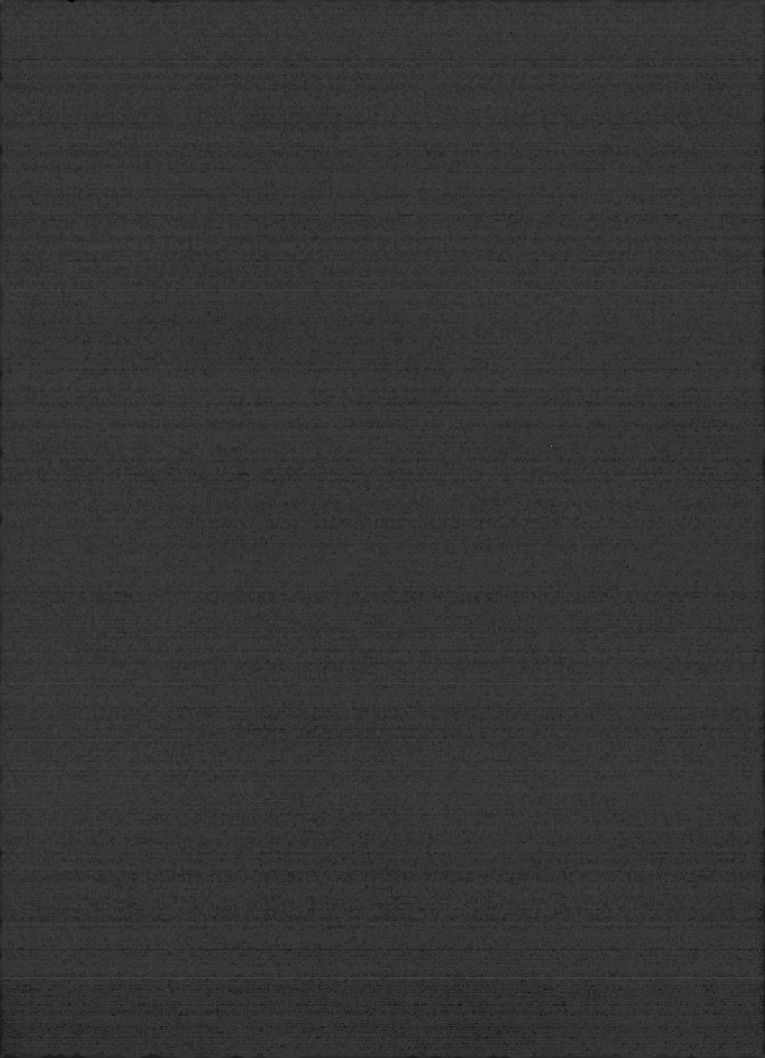

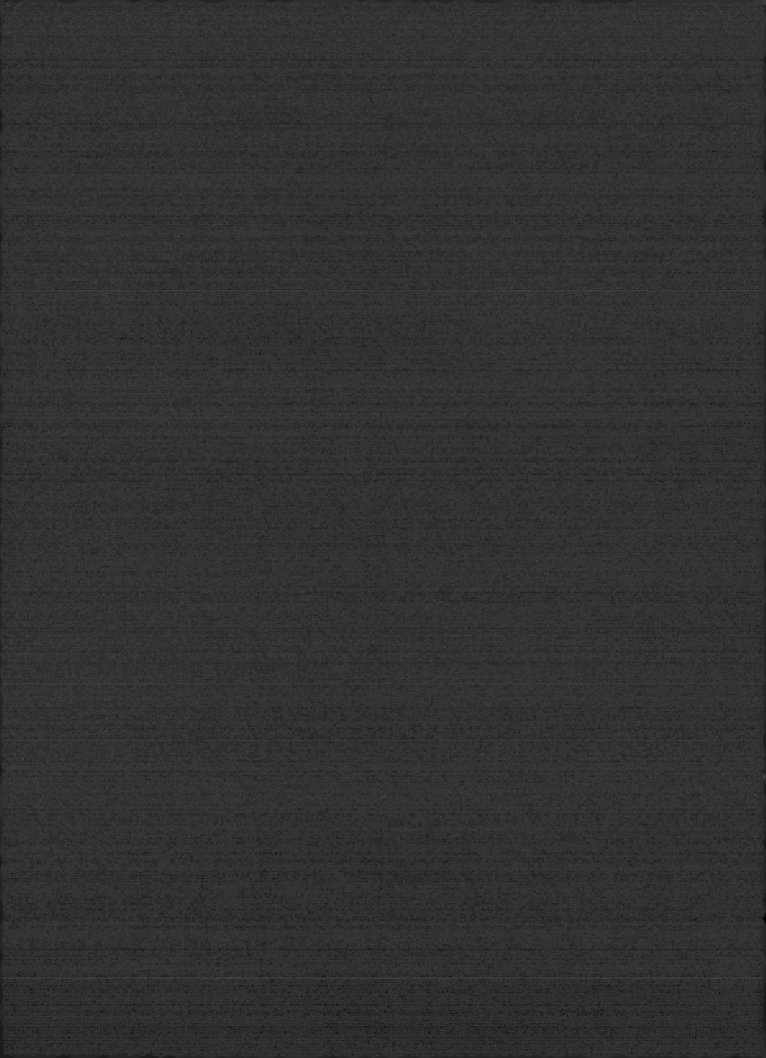

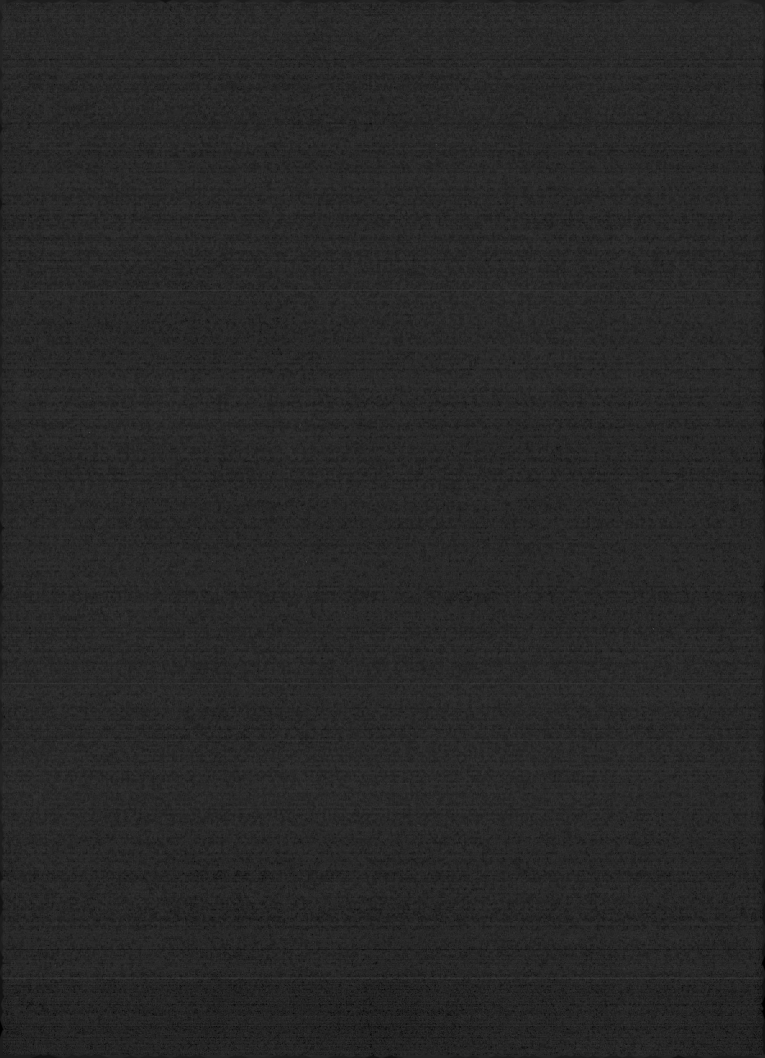

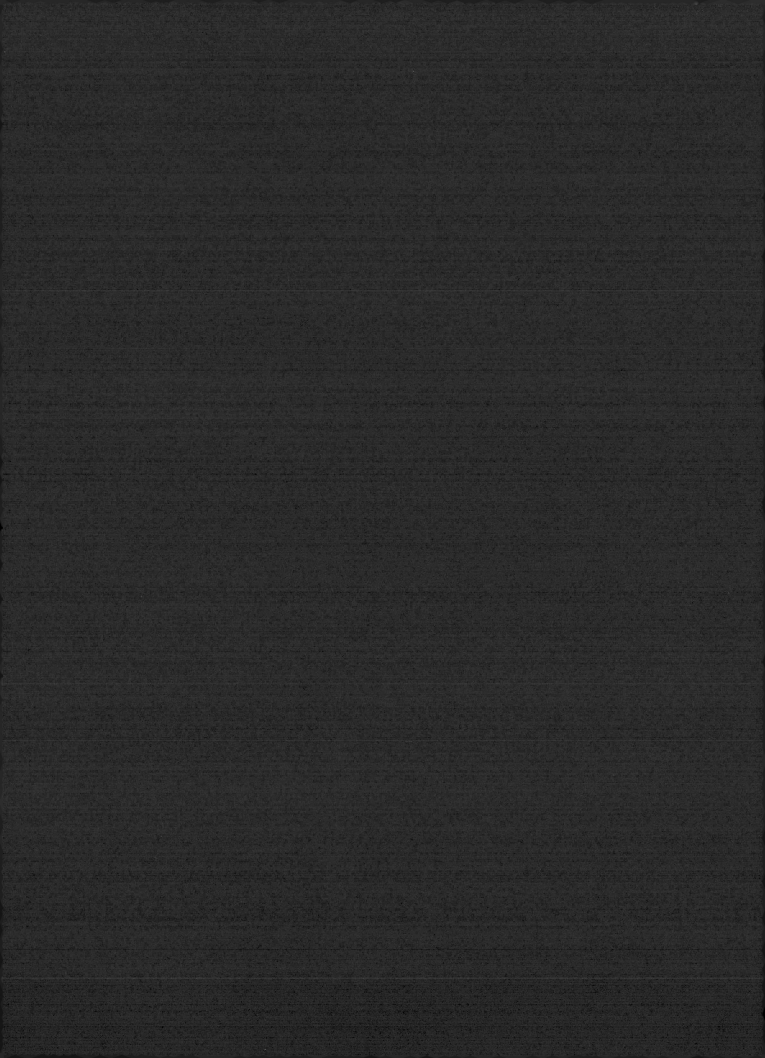

SPRING TIME

HAPPY AUTUMN

TRICK OR TREAT

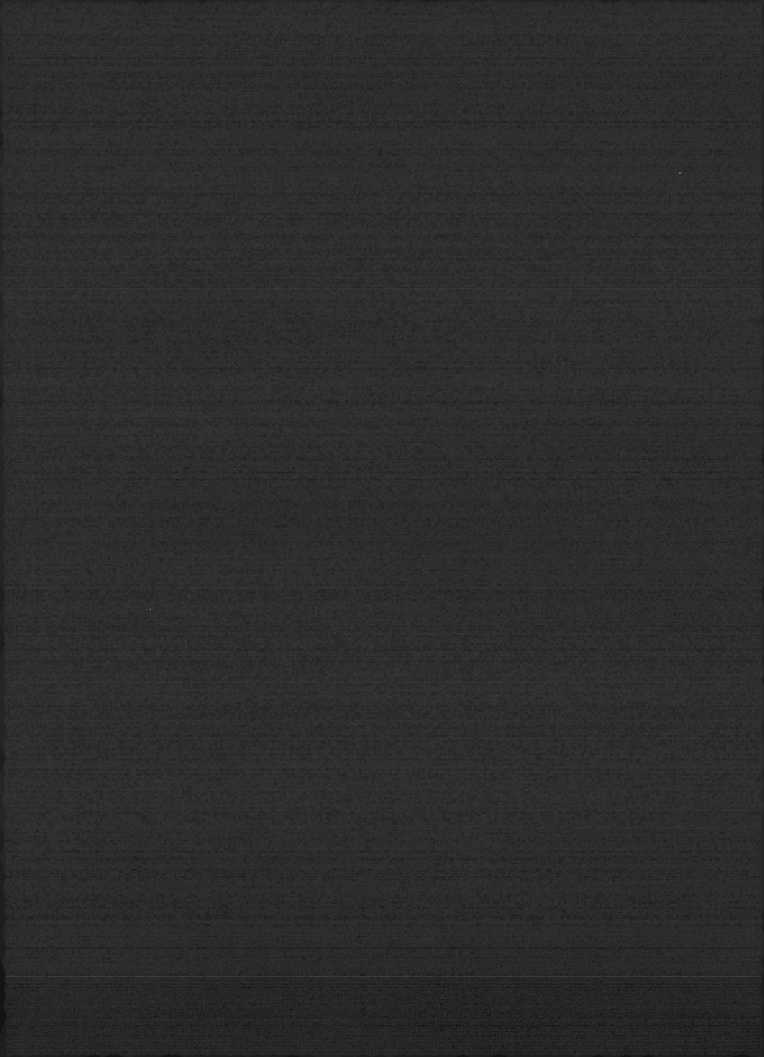

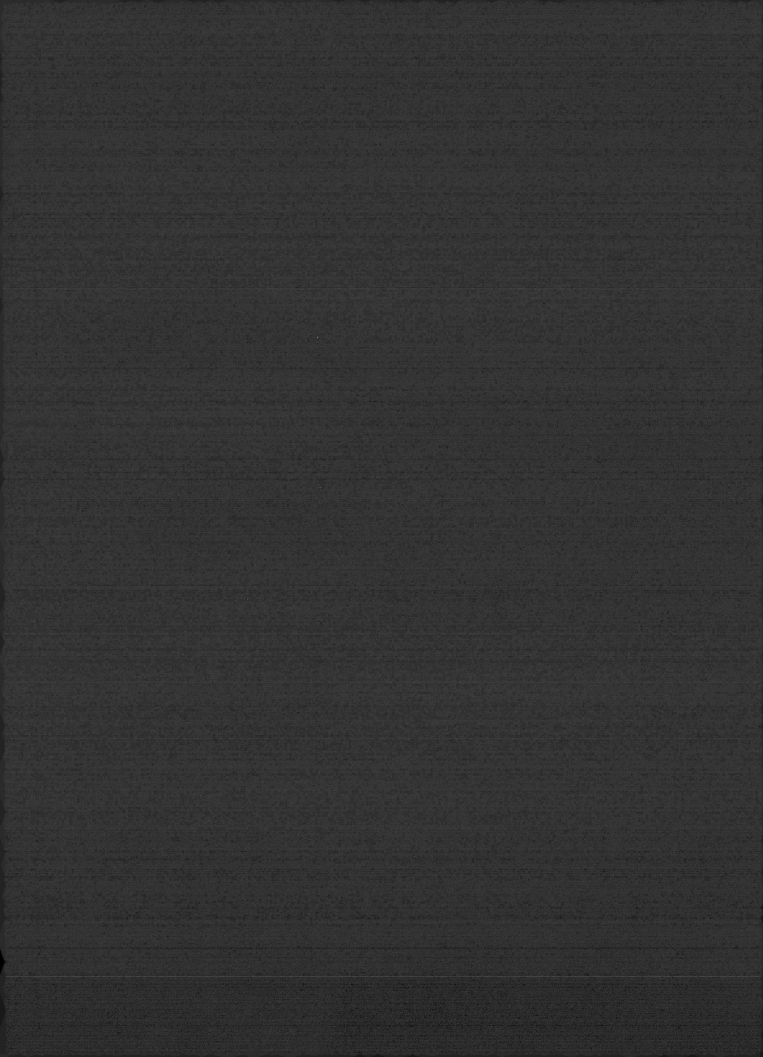

HELLO WINTER

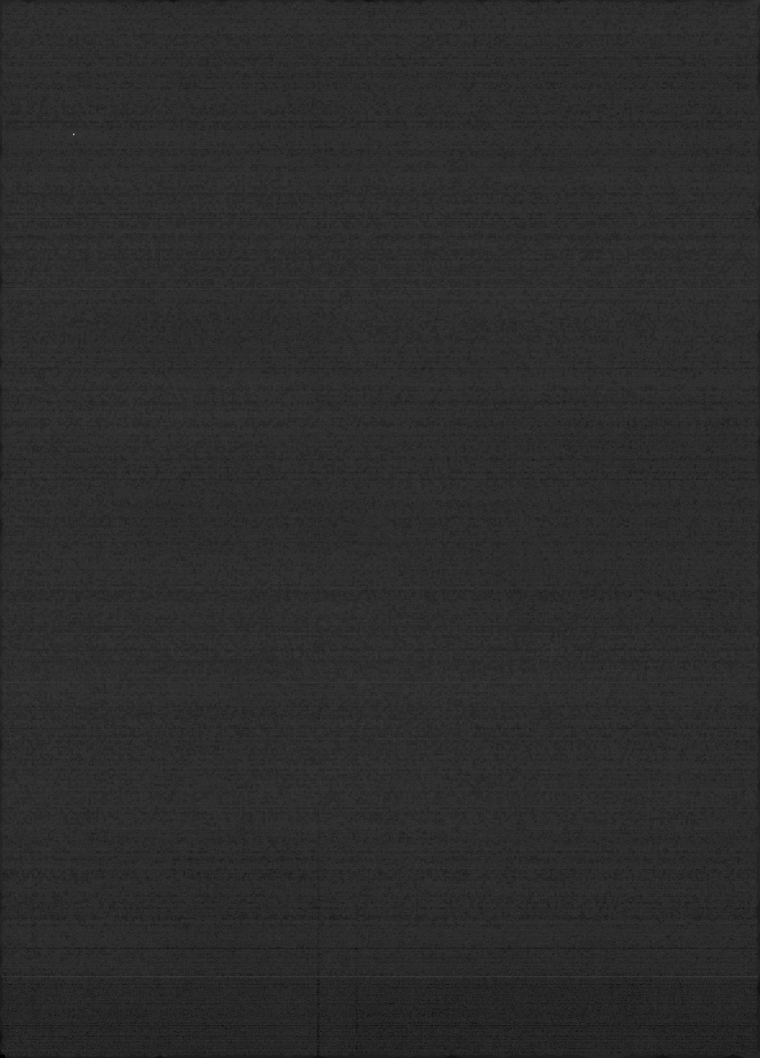

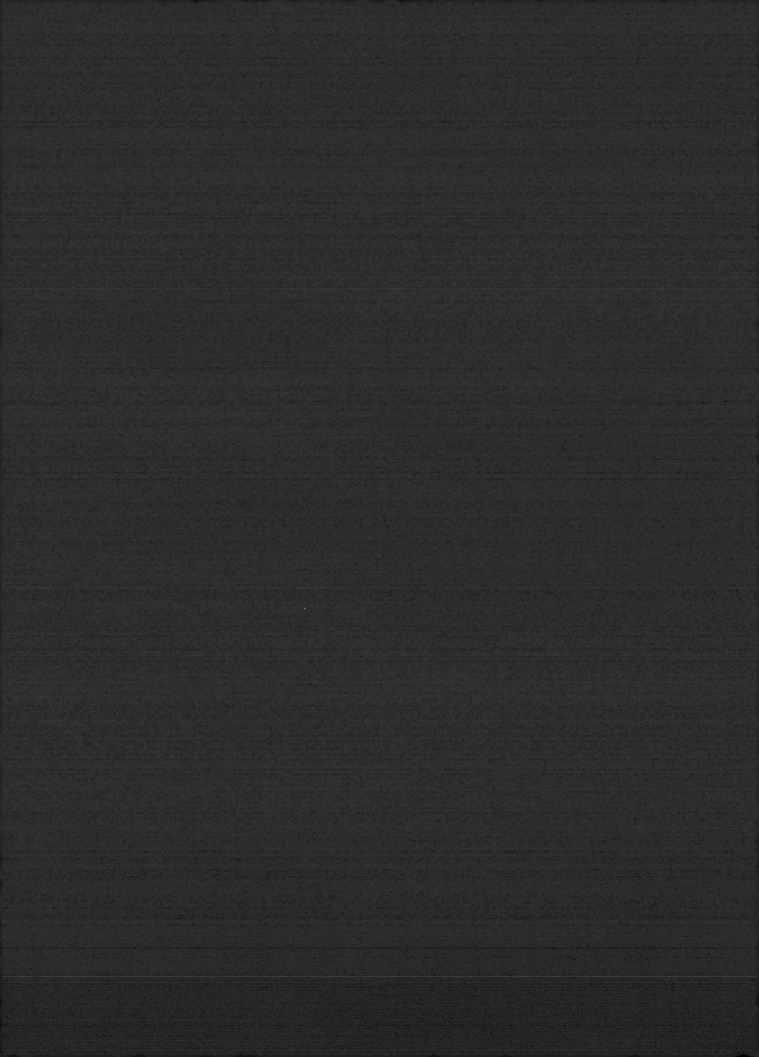

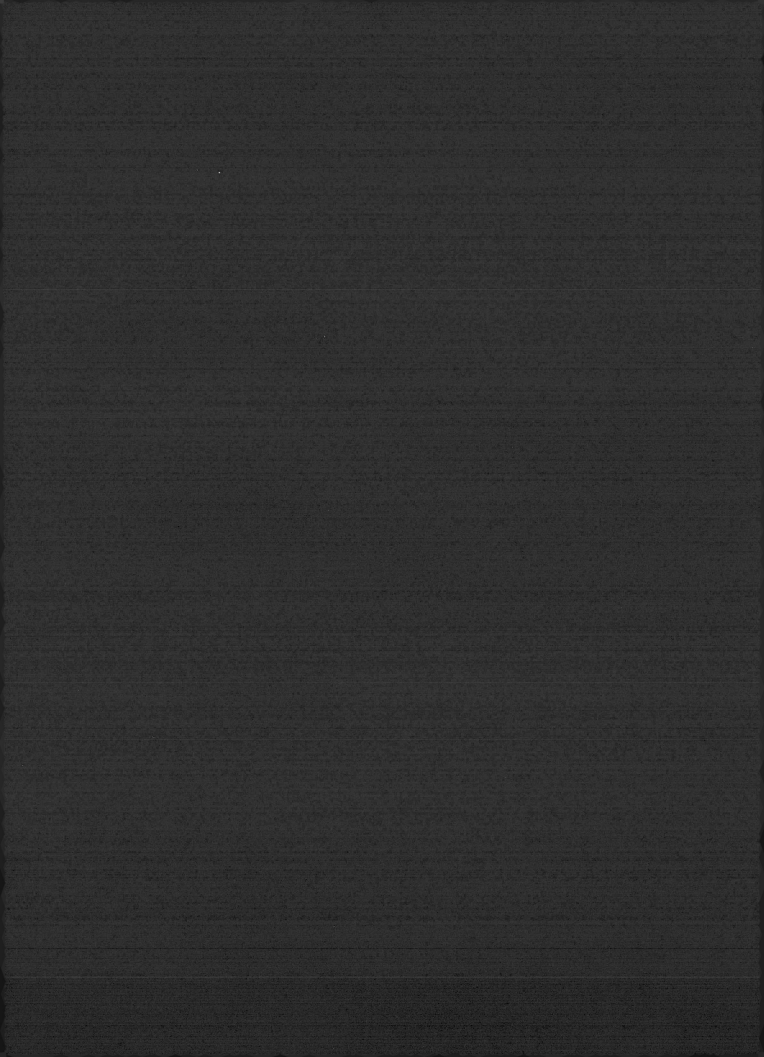

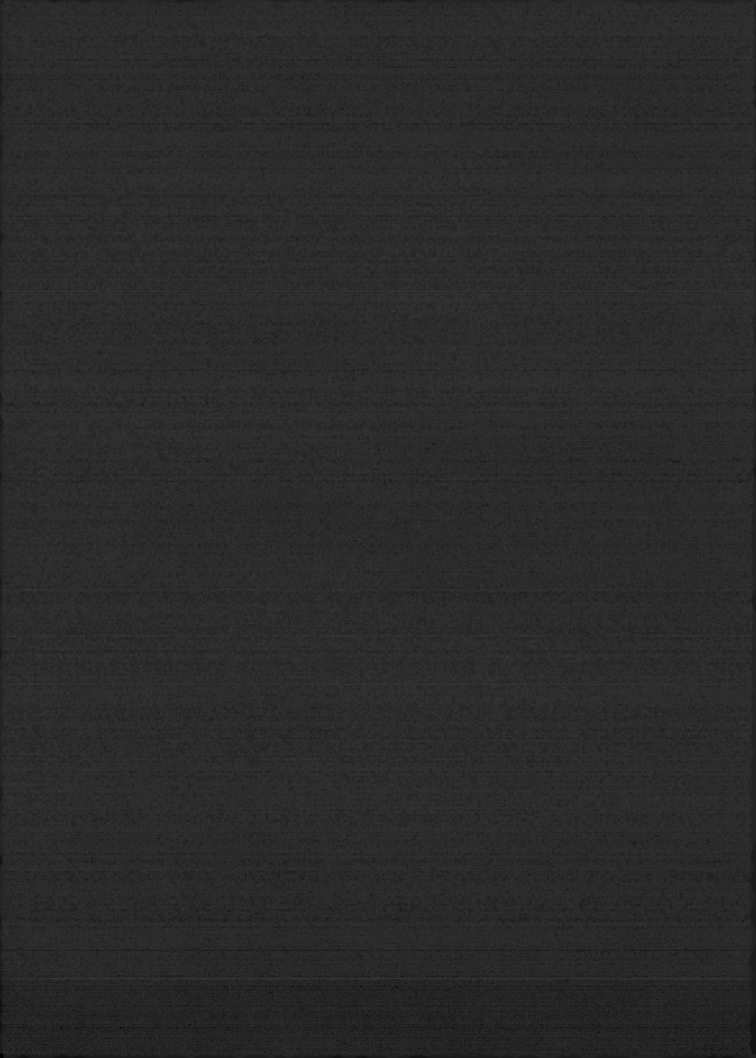

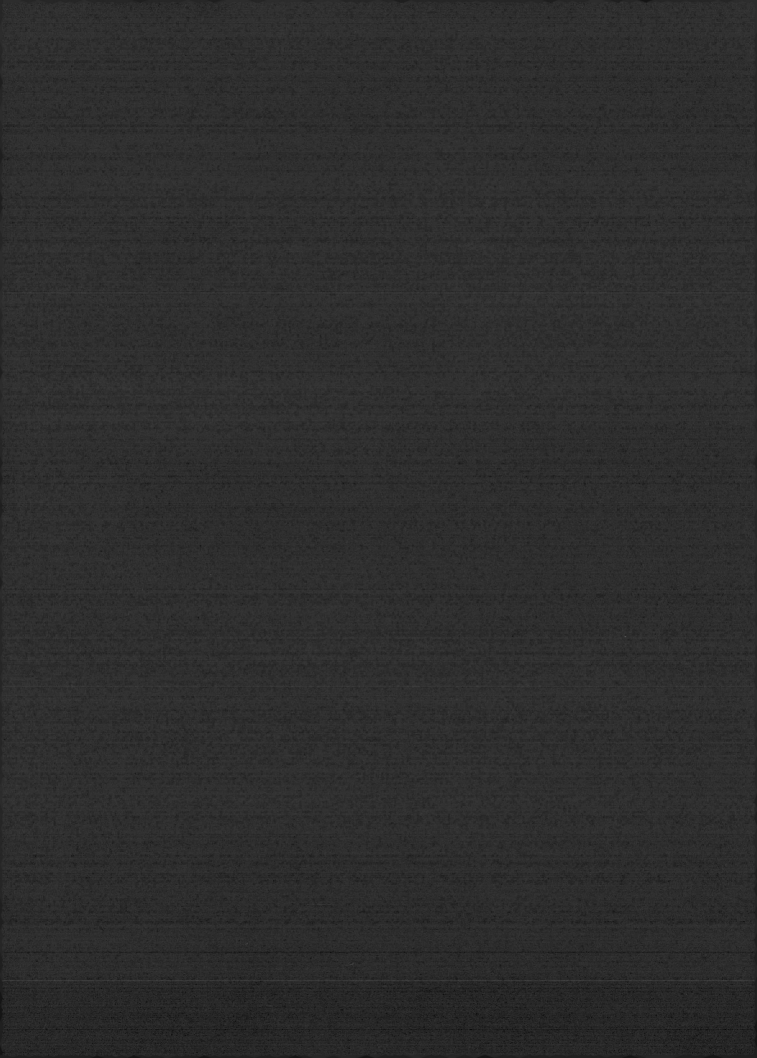

From the Author

Thank you for buying and coloring our book, we sincerely hope you have enjoyed it!

Can we ask for a small favor? A lot of work goes in to preparing and publishing our books and honest reviews really do help us, especially when it comes to understanding what we should improve in our books.

If you have a minute, we would really appreciate if you could just leave a review...we do actually read our reviews!

Thank you!

Bridget Coloring Press

DISCOVER THE BRIDGET COLORING PRESS COLLECTION

Discover the Bridget Coloring Collection of 100+ coloring books.

Bridget Coloring Press has an incredible variety of coloring books. We have something for everyone.

- Animals

- Beginners

- Flowers

- Funny

- Swear Words

- Holiday and Seasonal

- Inspirational

- Kids

- Mandalas and Patterns

- Nature

- Religious

- And More!

SCAN ME

We hope you enjoy your next Bridget Coloring Press book!

View the Bridget Coloring Press Collection :

https://www.amazon.com/Bridget-Coloring-Press/e/B0871PMK31

Printed in Great Britain
by Amazon

10214163R00119